I0817103

Spooky Spots

SPOOKY FORESTS & CAVES

ELSIE OLSON

Big Buddy Books

An Imprint of Abdo Publishing
abdobooks.com

abdobooks.com

Published by Abdo Publishing, a division of ABDO, PO Box 398166, Minneapolis, Minnesota 55439.

Printed in the United States of America, North Mankato, Minnesota
052020
092020

Design: Sarah DeYoung, Mighty Media, Inc.
Production: Mighty Media, Inc.
Editor: Rachael Thomas

Cover Photograph: iStockphoto
Interior Photographs: Library of Congress, p. 20; Neil Rickards/Wikimedia Commons, pp. 7 (Hellfire Caves), 15; Pixabay, pp. 7 (Black Forest), 23; Scott/Flickr, pp. 6 (Wabasha Street Caves), 25; Shutterstock Images, pp. 4–5, 6, 7, 10–11, 12, 13, 17, 18, 19, 21, 27, 28 (all), 29; Wikimedia Commons, p. 29 (backscatter); Www78/Wikimedia Commons, pp. 6 (Bell Witch Cave), 9
Design Elements: Shutterstock Images

Library of Congress Control Number: 2020931791

Publisher's Cataloging-in-Publication Data
Names: Olson, Elsie, author.
Title: Spooky forests & caves / by Elsie Olson
Description: Minneapolis, Minnesota : Abdo Publishing, 2021 | Series: Spooky spots | Includes online resources and index
Identifiers: ISBN 9781532193323 (lib. bdg.) | ISBN 9781098211967 (ebook)
Subjects: LCSH: Haunted places--Juvenile literature. | Ghosts--Juvenile literature. | Outdoor recreation areas--Juvenile literature. | Spirits--Juvenile literature.
Classification: DDC 133.12--dc23

CONTENTS

HAUNTED FORESTS AND CAVES

Do you believe there are ghosts among us? Many people do. Whether you're a believer or not, forests and caves are some of the spookiest spots around!

Get ready to **explore** some of the most haunted forests and caves on Earth. Walk among the twisted trees. Travel deep into dark caves. But look out! You may not be alone.

Forests are even spookier at night!

World's Spookiest

FORESTS AND CAVES

Are you ready for a ghostly adventure? Then pack up your wits and your **courage**. Let's take a trip to some of the world's spookiest forests and caves!

Hellfire Caves, England
Hoia Baciu Forest, Romania
Aokigahara Forest, Japan
Black Forest, Germany
RUSSIA
CHINA
INDIA
Indian Ocean

BELL WITCH CAVE

Bell Witch Cave is near Adams, Tennessee. The cave is on land that was owned by farmer John Bell in the 1800s. It is said that the ghost of a witch lived in the cave. She would come out to haunt Bell and his family.

Since then, some visitors say they hear voices in the cave. Pictures taken in the cave sometimes show ghostly figures and strange lights. It seems the Bell Witch may still call the cave home!

FRIGHTFUL FACT

US President Andrew Jackson once spent a night on Bell Farm. He said, “I had rather face the entire British Army than to spend another night with the Bell Witch.”

AOKIGAHARA FOREST

Aokigahara Forest is believed to be Japan's most haunted forest. It is near the **volcano** Mount Fuji. People call the forest *Jukai*. This is Japanese for "Sea of Trees."

Some of the trees are 300 years old. They stand so close together, the wind cannot blow through them. The forest is often spookily silent.

It is easy to get lost in Aokigahara Forest. Some hikers carry colored tape to mark the trail.

In Japanese **legends**, the forest is home to *yurei*. *Yurei* are said to be the ghosts of people who died suddenly or **violently**. These lost souls wander the forest and **lure** travelers off the paths.

FRIGHTFUL FACT

The soil in Aokigahara Forest has a lot of iron. This iron can stop cell phones from working properly.

Mount Fuji rises above Aokigahara Forest.

HELLFIRE CAVES

In the 1750s, Sir Francis Dashwood began an unusual **project**. He hired workers to dig caves beneath the hills of England's West Wycombe village.

Dashwood cofounded a group called the Hellfire Club. The club used the caves as a meeting place. To this day, no one knows what happened at their meetings.

Many people today believe the caves are haunted. Some have heard **chanting** deep inside the caves. Others have seen ghostly figures.

The Hellfire Caves are more than one-quarter mile (0.5 km) long.

THE PINE BARRENS

There is a huge forest in southern New Jersey called the Pine Barrens. It is a popular place for hiking, camping, and fishing. But people believe the forest is also home to the Jersey Devil!

It is said that the Jersey Devil was born in 1735. Since then, there have been strange sightings in the Pine Barrens. Screeches are heard at night. Pets and livestock go missing. Strange footprints are found in the snow.

FRIGHTFUL FACT

People say the Jersey Devil has a horse's face, a kangaroo's body, a pig's feet, a lizard's tail, and a bat's wings.

Native Americans named the Pine Barrens *Popuessing*. This means "place of the dragon."

MAMMOTH CAVE

Mammoth Cave is beneath the fields and forests of central Kentucky. It is the largest known cave system in the world.

Native Americans used Mammoth Cave for thousands of years. American settlers rediscovered the cave in 1790. More than 400 miles (644 km) of the cave have been **explored** since.

The Mammoth Cave area became a national park in 1941. Since then, visitors have reported more than 150 spooky happenings.

Explorers still haven't found an end to Mammoth Cave. No one knows how long it really is!

In the 1800s, Mammoth Cave was used as a hospital. So, many people believe the cave is haunted by former **patients**.

People have reported hearing footsteps and seeing strange figures inside the cave. Some even said they were pushed by an unseen force!

FRIGHTFUL FACT

African American slave Stephen Bishop was one of Mammoth Cave's earliest tour guides. Bishop died of an unknown illness in 1857. Some believe he haunts the cave today.

The main entrance to Mammoth Cave

THE BLACK FOREST

The Black Forest is in southwestern Germany. Trees in the forest stand so close together, light can barely get through. The forest is said to be home to witches, **werewolves**, and ghosts.

One **legend** is really spooky. Locals tell stories of a tall, thin man who lives in the forest. The man has large eyes and a scary face. He steals **naughty** children who enter the forest.

FRIGHTFUL FACT

The story of Hansel and Gretel is set in the Black Forest. In the story, two children wander into the forest and are taken by a witch!

The Black Forest covers 2,320 square miles (6,009 sq km).

WABASHA STREET CAVES

The Wabasha Street Caves were created in the early 1900s. They were dug into the rocky hills on the shores of the Mississippi River in Minnesota.

At first, people stored supplies and grew **mushrooms** in the caves. But in the 1930s, the caves were turned into a **nightclub**. It became a popular hangout for **gangsters**.

Today, people still visit the caves to eat, drink, and listen to music. But many people report seeing the ghosts of gangsters. Some even say they took pictures of the ghosts!

The bar area is said to be one of the most haunted areas of the Wabasha Street Caves.

HOIA BACIU FOREST

The Transylvania area of Romania is the setting for many **vampire** stories. But Transylvania is also home to haunted forest Hoia Baciu. The forest is only about one square mile (3 sq km). Some locals are afraid to enter it.

People have reported seeing **UFOs**, balls of light, and shadowy figures in Hoia Baciu. Visitors also reported feeling as if something were watching them.

FRIGHTFUL FACT

There is an area in the middle of Hoia Baciu Forest where no trees grow. Some people believe this is a gateway to another world.

Hoia Baciu Forest is said to be named after a shepherd who disappeared in the forest many years ago.

SPOOKY OR SCIENCE?

You've just learned about some spooky forests and caves. The creepy stories are fun! But good **explorers** look for reasons for what they see and hear. Strange happenings can often be explained by science.

Do you think the forests and caves in this book are actually haunted? You might have to visit them to find out!

IMAGINATION

Humans have excellent imaginations. Just hearing about a scary sight can trick your brain into thinking you've seen it too!

MISTAKEN IDENTITY

In low light, it can be easy to mistake familiar creatures for strange monsters! The Jersey Devil sightings could have been large birds or deer.

EXAGGERATION

Tourist sites may exaggerate spooky stories. They hope this will make more people want to visit.

SPOOKY PICTURES

Many visitors to haunted places report balls of light in their pictures. These are likely backscatter. Backscatter is when a camera's flash lights up specks of dust or water.

GLOSSARY

chant – to repeat a word or phrase to a beat. Usually, chants are spoken loudly by a crowd.

courage – strength or bravery.

exaggerate (ihg-ZA-juh-rayt) – to make something seem larger or more impressive.

explore – to go into in order to make a discovery or to have an adventure. A person who explores is an explorer.

gangster – a member of a group of criminals.

legend – an old story that many people believe but cannot be proven true.

lure – to cause a person or an animal to go somewhere by offering some pleasure or gain.

mushroom – an umbrella-shaped fungus. Some mushrooms are used in cooking.

naughty (NAW-tee) – behaving in a bad or improper way.

nightclub – a place where people can eat, drink, and dance.

patient (PAY-shehnt) – a person who is under the care of a doctor.

project – a task or activity.

speck – a tiny dot or particle.

tourist site – a place people visit while on vacation.

UFO – an abbreviation for "unidentified flying object."

vampire – a made-up monster that is a dead person who comes out at night to suck the blood of living people.

violently – with or due to a strong physical force.

volcano – a deep opening in Earth's surface from which hot liquid rock or steam comes out.

werewolf – a person who can take the form of a wolf.

ONLINE RESOURCES

To learn more about spooky forests and caves, please visit **abdobooklinks.com** or scan this QR code. These links are routinely monitored and updated to provide the most current information available.

INDEX